TREES

COTTONWOOD TREES

John F. Prevost
ABDO & Daughters

Published by Abdo & Daughters, 4940 Viking Drive, Suite 622, Edina, Minnesota 55435.

Copyright © 1996 by Abdo Consulting Group, Inc., Pentagon Tower, P.O. Box 36036, Minneapolis, Minnesota 55435 USA. International copyrights reserved in all countries. No part of this book may be reproduced in any form without written permission from the publisher.

Printed in the United States.

Cover Photo credits: Peter Arnold, Inc.
Interior Photo credits: Peter Arnold, Inc.

Edited by Bob Italia

Library of Congress Cataloging-in-Publication Data

Prevost, John F.
    Cottonwood Trees / John F. Prevost.
      p. cm. -- (Trees)
    Includes index.
    Summary: Provides basic information about the cottonwood, including its structure, economic uses, and the pests and diseases that affect it.
      ISBN 1-56239-615-3
    1. Cottonwood--Juvenile literature. [1. Apples.] I. Title. II. Series: Prevost, John F.
    Trees.
    QK495.S16P74 1996   96-6068
    583'.981--dc20   CIP
                                                                        AC

ABOUT THE AUTHOR
John Prevost is a marine biologist and diver who has been active in conservation and education issues for the past 18 years. Currently he is living inland and remains actively involved in freshwater and marine husbandry, conservation and education projects.

Contents

Cottonwood Trees and Family

Cottonwoods are large trees that may grow over 100 feet (30 meters) tall. They are named for the cotton-like hairs attached to their seeds. When the seeds drop from the trees, they coat everything with this fiber. Cottonwood trees are from North America. They are also called **poplars.**

Cottonwoods are **deciduous** trees. Their leaves fall off in the autumn. They grow from seeds or **cuttings**.

Cottonwood trees have cotton-like hairs that grow from their seeds.

Roots, Soil, and Water

Cottonwood trees pull water from the ground with their roots. **Minerals** and other **nutrients** are in the water. These are the food for the tree. Without enough food, the tree will not grow or make seeds. The roots also keep the tree from falling over.

Cottonwoods and other **poplars** grow near water. These trees can live in dry areas. They have a long root system to find water. But these roots can clog sewers and other water drains. Like **willows**, cottonwoods should not be planted close to sewers.

Opposite page:
Cottonwoods have long roots
which help find groundwater.

Stems, Leaves, and Sunlight

Sunlight is important to every green plant. The tree uses sunlight to change water, **nutrients**, and air into plant food and **oxygen**. This process is called **photosynthesis**.

The cottonwood's trunk holds up the branches, stems, and leaves. It also connects the roots to the leaves. This allows water to reach the leaves where food is made. The food then travels to the roots.

The branches and stems are long and **brittle**. In high winds, branches are easily broken. These trees should not be planted close to buildings.

Most cottonwood leaves are triangular-shaped. Their edges are jagged. The **leafstalks** are long and flattened, and allow the leaves to flutter in a breeze.

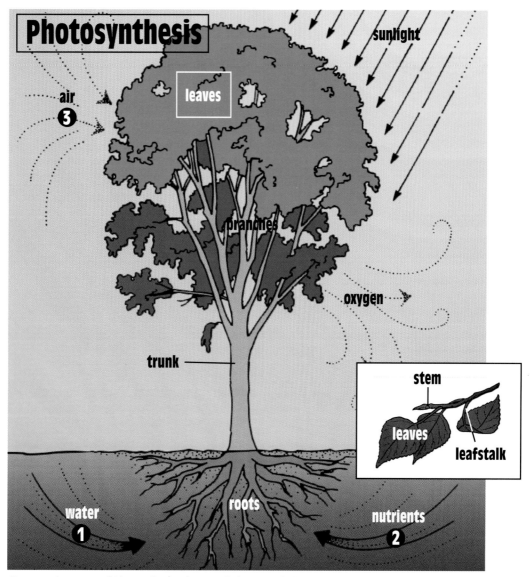

Photosynthesis

sunlight

air ❸

leaves

branches

oxygen

trunk

stem

leaves

leafstalk

water ❶

roots

nutrients ❷

Ground water (1) and nutrients (2) travel through the roots, trunk, and branches and into the leaves where air (3) is drawn in. Then the tree uses sunlight to change these three elements into food and oxygen.

9

Flowers and Seeds

Cottonwoods and other **poplars** flower in the spring. The male and female flowers are on separate trees. The male flowers are called **staminate.** The female flowers are called **pistillate.**

The fruit on cottonwoods are small, rarely over 1.5 inches (4 cm) long. The seeds are released from the fruits when ripe.

The seeds are very small, some are less than 1.5 inches (4 cm) long. The hairs act as parachutes, slowing the fall of the seeds. Any wind will carry them far away.

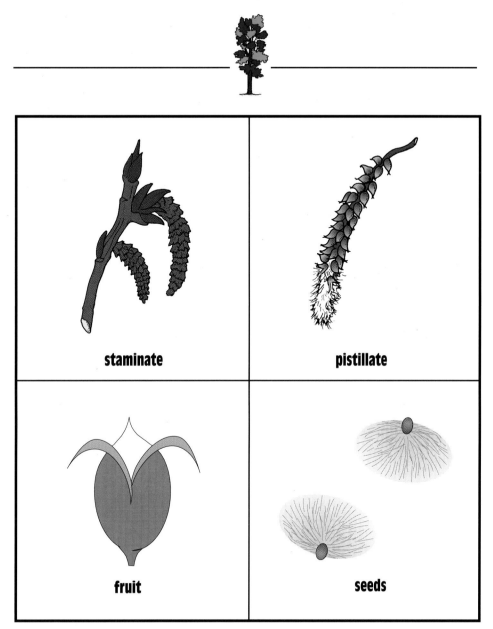

staminate	**pistillate**
fruit	**seeds**

The staminate makes pollen that fertilizes the pistillate.
The pistillate grows fruit which make seeds.

Insects and Other Friends

Cottonwood trees are home to hundreds of insects, spiders, and **mites**. Most help the tree live a healthy life. Many insects carry **pollen** from flower to flower, **fertilizing** them.

Many types of birds nest in cottonwood trees.

Cottonwoods are home for birds and small **mammals**. Many nest in the tree and feed **pests** to their young. Others use the tree for shelter.

Nesting birds include wrens, robins, and sparrows. Nesting mammals are squirrels, chipmunks, and bats.

Many animals seek shelter in cottonwood trees.

Pests and Diseases

Cottonwood trees do not last more than 25 to 30 years. Many insects such as **aphids**, **thrips**, **scale**, caterpillars, and beetles like to eat these trees. Healthy trees can resist these **pests.** But **drought** or storm damage will weaken them.

Ladybugs and other predatory insects eat pests.

Sprays can kill many chewing insects. **Predatory** insects, like ladybugs and wasps, can be used to control other insect pests. **Diseases** also attack weak cottonwood trees.

Many birds and **mammals** like to eat cottonwood buds and bark. Rabbits, deer, beaver, and bear include the buds and twigs in their diet. Birds such as ruffled grouse and prairie chicken also feed on the seeds and buds.

Birds and mammals feed on the buds and bark of cottonwoods.

Varieties

There are many types of cottonwood trees. Most people like a non-messy tree when they buy one. One type is called Siouxland. Only male trees are sold. They have darker leaves, and can fight disease.

Varieties are sold because they are stronger and can survive harsh weather, or because they are pleasant to look at.

Opposite page: Cottonwood and sycamore trees near Montezuma's Castle, New Mexico.

Uses

Cottonwoods and other **poplars** are fast-growing trees. They are often planted for wind protection, **erosion** control, quick shade, or as a temporary tree until other, more long-lived trees, can grow.

Their soft wood is used to make paper, **veneers**, chopsticks, and matches. Trees that are cut down will often recover by sending **shoots** up from their shallow roots. Within 7 to 12 years, a second **harvest** is possible from the same site.

Opposite page:
Cottonwoods are fast-growing
trees and often planted for
erosion control.

Cottonwood Trees and the Plant Kingdom

The plant kingdom is divided into several groups, including flowering plants, fungi, plants with bare seeds, and ferns.

 Flowering plants grow flowers to make seeds. These seeds often grow inside protective ovaries or fruit.

 Fungi are plants without leaves, flowers, or green coloring, and cannot make their own food. They include mushrooms, molds, and yeast.

 Plants with bare seeds (such as evergreens, conifers) do not grow flowers. Their seeds grow unprotected, often on the scale of a cone.

 Ferns are plants with roots, stems, and leaves. They do not grow flowers or seeds.

There are two groups of flowering plants: monocots (MAH-no-cots) and dicots (DIE-cots). Monocots have seedlings with one leaf. Dicots have seedlings with two leaves.

The Willow and Poplar family is one type of dicot. Cottonwood trees belong to the Willow and Poplar family.

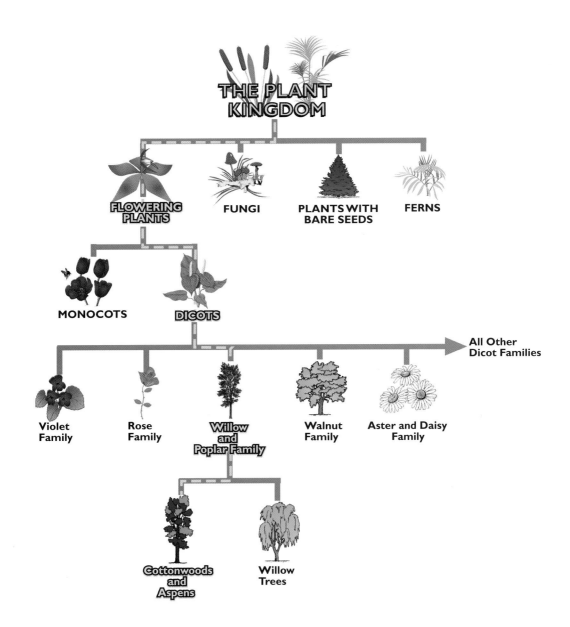

THE PLANT KINGDOM

FLOWERING PLANTS

FUNGI

PLANTS WITH BARE SEEDS

FERNS

MONOCOTS

DICOTS

Violet Family

Rose Family

Willow and Poplar Family

Walnut Family

Aster and Daisy Family

All Other Dicot Families

Cottonwoods and Aspens

Willow Trees

Glossary

aphid (AY-fid) - A small, soft-bodied insect that damages plants by sucking the juices from leaves and stems.

brittle - Very easily broken.

cutting - A piece that has been cut off and replanted.

deciduous (duh-SID-yoo-us) - Trees which lose their leaves in the fall.

disease - A sickness.

drought (DROWT) - A long period of dry weather.

erosion (ear-OH-zun) - Being worn away little by little.

fertilize (FUR-tuh-lize) - To make a thing start to grow.

harvest - To cut down and gather crops or trees.

leafstalk - A slender stem that supports a leaf.

mammal (MAM-ull) - A class of animals, including humans, that have hair and feed their young milk.

mineral (MIN-er-ull) - Any substance that is not a plant, animal, or another living thing.

mite - A tiny animal related to the spider that has eight legs.

nutrient (NEW-tree-ent) - A substance that promotes growth or good health.

oxygen (OX-ih-jen) - A gas without color, taste, or odor that is found in the air and water.

pest - A harmful or destructive insect or animal.

photosynthesis (foe-toe-SIN-thuh-sis) - Producing food using sunlight as the source of energy.

pistillate (PIS-till-ate) - The part of a flower that makes seeds.

pollen (PAH-len) - A fine, yellow powder that fertilizes flowers.

pollinate (PAH-lin-ate) - To move pollen from flower to flower, allowing them to develop seeds.

poplar (POP-lirr) - A tree that grows rapidly and produces light, soft wood.

predator (PRED-uh-tore) - An animal that eats other animals.

scale - A small soft-bodied insect that resembles small scales as it rests on plants.

shoot - A young branch.

staminate (STAM-ih-nate) - The part of a flower that makes pollen.

thrip - A soft-bodied insect that feeds on plants.

variety (vuh-RYE-uh-tee) - A number of different kinds.

veneer (vuh-NEER) - A thin layer of wood used to decorate or protect a surface.

willow - A tree with tough, slender branches and narrow leaves.

Index